# THE SOUTHERN AROUND LONDON
## A Colour Portfolio

Ian Allan
PUBLISHING

Kevin McCormack

# Introduction

The Southern was different from other Regions. It had no long-distance rail services and no water troughs, and most of its trains were electric. But what a wonderful variety of steam locomotives it had, even in the early 1960s; many of them were pre-Grouping, some even Victorian.

The Southern Railway of 1923 was an amalgamation of the London & South Western Railway (whose locomotive designers included Beattie, Drummond and Urie), the London, Brighton & South Coast Railway (Marsh and Billinton) and the South Eastern & Chatham Railway (Wainwright and Maunsell). The last was in fact a joint committee of two separate legal entities — the South Eastern Railway and the London, Chatham & Dover Railway. The Southern Railway had two locomotive designers between 1923 and Nationalisation in 1948: Maunsell (from the SECR) and then Bulleid.

I was brought up on the Western Region near Ealing Broadway and had little opportunity to visit the Southern during my childhood except when visiting my school outfitters at Sloane Square. Then I would drag my mother into Victoria station so that I could train-spot and admire the 'Golden Arrow' (if it was there). I obtained my first

*Above:* Resembling the ill-fated 'River' class and reputedly incorporating the tanks and other parts of these locomotives, the 'W' class 2-6-4 tanks were designed for cross-Region freights. On one such working, No 31925 was found at Willesden on 2 February 1963. *Geoff Rixon*

*Previous page:* An up Ramsgate excursion formed of narrow Hastings-line stock approaches Shortlands Junction on 4 August 1957. At the head is 'Schools' class 4-4-0 No 30909 *St Paul's. Ken Wightman*

*Front cover:* Shadows are lengthening at Betchworth as 'N' class No 31862 arrives with a Redhill–Reading train in the summer of 1962. This attractive station survives today and retains original spiral-column lamps on the platforms. *Nick Lera*

*Back cover:* The '82xxx' Standard tanks arrived at Nine Elms (now the site of New Covent Garden market) from November 1962 to take over empty stock workings at Waterloo. Nos 82025 and 82016 bask in the evening sun in October 1963. *Marcus Eavis*

First published 2003

ISBN 0 7110 2968 7

© Kevin R. McCormack 2003

Published by Ian Allan Publishing

an imprint of Ian Allan Publishing Ltd, Hersham, Surrey KT12 4RG.
Printed by Ian Allan Printing Ltd, Hersham, Surrey KT12 4RG.

Code: 0302/B2

'footplate' at Victoria — an elderly 'D' class 4-4-0, No 31574, which was being used on empty-stock duties. I couldn't get over how huge the cab was; it could have accommodated over a dozen small schoolboys!

During the 1960s (after I had discarded my mother!), I attended various 'last days' of steam on the Southern: the closure of the Westerham branch and the Guildford–Horsham line, the end of steam on the Reading–Redhill line, the final run of the last 'S15' and, of course, the very last day of steam on the Southern — 9 July 1967.

*The Southern around London* is a reminder of the two-stage replacement of steam on the Kent lines on 14 June 1959 and 11 June 1961, the end of Central Division suburban steam on 13 June 1965 and steam's grand finale on the Waterloo–Bournemouth line. The term 'around London' should not be taken too literally, although Southern steam could be seen regularly at such diverse locations as Oxford and Willesden Junction and sometimes on 'foreign' sheds such as Neasden. (I remember 'copping' No 30777 *Sir Lamiel* as it seemed to emerge from the ground at Cricklewood.) As far as proximity to London is concerned, virtually all the photographs were taken within a 35-mile radius of the capital.

The splendid colour images in this book, only a few of which I can take credit for, vividly portray main-line, suburban and branch-line steam operation in its final 10 years. I am very grateful to the following photographers for letting me use their precious transparencies: Geoff Rixon, David Clark (his own and the late Ken Wightman's), Marcus Eavis, Nick Lera (of video fame), Jim Oatway, Derek Penney, Bruce Jenkins, Roy Hobbs and Martin Jenkins. Some of these names will be familiar to readers of my Ian Allan bus albums — what a versatile bunch they are! Thanks go also to Judith Barnes for her map-reading skills during location checking.

Finally, although there are some unfortunate omissions in the ranks of preserved Southern steam (such as the LBSCR 'K' class Moguls and the rebuilt SECR 4-4-0s), representatives of most classes featured in this title have been preserved and, in some cases, in quite large numbers, thanks mainly to the late Dai Woodham's legendary scrapyard at Barry in South Wales. Many of them can be found on the Bluebell, Kent & East Sussex, Mid-Hants and Swanage railways, for example. I hope that this book will whet the appetite of readers to seek out the survivors and support their restoration, upkeep and operation.

*Kevin R. McCormack*
Ashtead, Surrey
October 2002

*Right:* Built between 1951 and 1957, the Standard Class 4 tanks were versatile engines but not often seen on long freight trains like No 80143 at Esher on 11 March 1965. *Geoff Rixon*

*Left:* Following the strengthening of the Kent main line, 22 powerful engines of the 'L' class were built in 1914. Viewed from the signalbox on 24 May 1958, No 31772, built in Berlin (surprisingly, given the date), leaves Tonbridge on a Brighton train composed of 'birdcage' stock. *Ken Wightman*

*Above:* Eighty 'N' class 2-6-0s were built between 1917 and 1934. No 31824, dating from 1923, pulls an up Brighton–Victoria train out of Eridge in March 1962. Services on this line now terminate at Uckfield. *David Clark*

*Left:* All 30 'Merchant Navy' Pacifics had their streamlining removed from 1956 onwards. In rebuilt form, No 35007 *Aberdeen Commonwealth* leaves Clapham Junction on a down express in September 1966. *Nick Lera*

*Above:* Returning briefly to their old stamping-ground after an absence of over 60 years, Beattie 2-4-0 well tanks Nos 30585 and 30587 (both now preserved) depart from Waterloo on 2 December 1962. Originating in 1863, all but three of this 88-strong class had been withdrawn by 1900. *Bruce Jenkins*

*Above:* Standard Class 5 4-6-0 No 73171, the last member of the class, heads an up express towards Bramshot, between Fleet and Farnborough, in August 1965. Some of the class received names from withdrawn 'King Arthurs'. *Author*

*Right:* A push-and-pull train to East Grinstead prepares to leave Three Bridges behind SECR 'H' class 0-4-4 tank No 31005 in the summer of 1962. This line was steam-operated until 4 January 1964 and was closed to passengers on 2 November 1967. *Marcus Eavis*

*Left:* LSWR 'M7' class 0-4-4 tank No 30032 shunts at Kingston in April 1963. Between 1896 and 1911, 105 members of this class were built, two of which have survived the cutter's torch. *Geoff Rixon*

*Above:* The 'Lord Nelsons' were among the most powerful 4-6-0s ever built. Constructed in 1928, No 30857 *Lord Howe* was photographed on the Western Region at Tilehurst, near Reading, in the summer of 1962. *Derek Penney*

*Above:* Maunsell 'S15' 4-6-0 No 30837 backs into Feltham shed in August 1965. This locomotive went on to become the last active member of the class. *Author*

*Right:* An Oxted–Tunbridge Wells West train is propelled past High Rocks by 'H' class tank No 31278 on 4 November 1961. The Spa Valley Railway now operates along this route. *Nick Lera*

*Above:* Wainwright's 'H' class passenger tank locomotive was a particularly successful design, giving 60 years' service. In all, 66 were built between 1904 and 1915. No 31518, photographed in the summer of 1959 at Maidstone West on a Tonbridge service, dates from 1908. *Marcus Eavis*

*Right:* The LSWR's '700' class of 30 goods locomotives had an even longer innings, having been designed by Drummond and introduced in 1897. No 30346 has just arrived at Woking on a freight from Feltham on 20 July 1962. *Geoff Rixon*

*Left:* The most powerful British 4-4-0 was the 40-strong 'Schools' class, designed primarily for the limited clearances and steep gradients of the Tonbridge–Hastings line. Here on the South Western in July 1962 is No 30925 *Cheltenham* (one of three now preserved) approaching Walton-on-Thames. *Geoff Rixon*

*Above:* 'King Arthur' class 4-6-0 No 30798 *Sir Hectimere* approaches Esher on a down Basingstoke train in December 1961. Despite its presentable appearance, the locomotive is only six months away from withdrawal. *Geoff Rixon*

*Above:* Looking as grimy as it did on page 1, 'Schools' class 4-4-0 No 30909 *St Paul's* speeds towards Petts Wood Junction in April 1956 on a Charing Cross–Hastings express. *David Clark*

*Right:* An Oxted–Tunbridge Wells West train propelled by SECR 'H' class 0-4-4 tank No 31005 stands at Goombridge station in June 1963. The Spa Valley Railway has built a new station nearby but this one still stands, in pristine condition, in private hands. *David Clark*

*Above:* A down excursion to Margate leaves Bromley South behind 'D1' class 4-4-0 No 31505 on 4 August 1957. There were 51 members of the earlier 'D' class, 21 of which were rebuilt as 'D1s' between 1921 and 1927. *Ken Wightman*

*Right:* Last days of the Guildford–Horsham line in June 1965 as LMS-designed Ivatt 2-6-2 tank No 41301 approaches Baynards Tunnel. This former LBSCR branch missed its centenary by four months. *Roy Hobbs*

*Above:* No trace remains of this scene at Grange Road station (near Crawley Down) on the Three Bridges–East Grinstead line. Houses in aptly named Old Station Close now stand where, on 16 March 1963, 'H' class tank No 31551 waits at the platform. *Geoff Rixon*

*Right:* Standard 2-6-4 tank No 80081 arrives at Edenbridge in 1964 on a Redhill–Tonbridge local. The 'economy' SER wooden buildings and 'budget' lamp standard and signs have been swept away and the board crossing between the staggered platforms has been replaced by a footbridge. *Nick Lera*

*Above:* A different perspective of the South Western main line at Esher shows 'King Arthur' class 4-6-0 No 30763 *Sir Bors de Ganis* heading a down train shortly before withdrawal in October 1960. *Geoff Rixon*

*Right:* Hauling a troop train, 'Schools' class No 30922 *Marlborough* brings a rake of Eastern Region stock into Willesden Junction (High Level) on 31 July 1960. *Geoff Rixon*

*Below:* A view of a line which operated for less than 30 years. Allhallows-on-Sea, on the Thames Estuary, failed to become a major resort, and the station was closed on 4 December 1961. 'H' class No 31530 sets off for Gravesend on 25 November 1961, leaving behind a railway scene now vanished apart from the water tower, which miraculously survives among mobile homes and caravans. *Ken Wightman*

*Right:* The last steam-hauled Pullman train in Britain was the 12.30pm departure from Waterloo, better known as the 'Bournemouth Belle'. This view from the footbridge west of Wimbledon station depicts the down 'Belle' in the hands of rebuilt 'Merchant Navy' No 35013 *Blue Funnel*. Eleven of the class of 30 survive. *Author's collection*

*Left:* On the last day of steam on the former SER Reading–Redhill line, 3 January 1965, 'U' class 2-6-0 No 31627 awaits the 'right away' at Reading Southern station (now a car park). *Author*

*Right:* 'King Arthur' class No 30451 *Sir Lamorak* takes the down slow line at Weybridge with a Waterloo–Basingstoke train in April 1962. This locomotive, designed by Maunsell, was built at Eastleigh in June 1925 and was withdrawn exactly 37 years later. Fortunately, one member of the class survives — No 30777 *Sir Lamiel.* 54 Maunsell 'King Arthurs' ('N15s') were built and 20 earlier Urie machines were added to the class and named. In due course these were modified to Maunsell's improved standards. *Geoff Rixon*

*Above:* The 45 members of the 'S15' class were designed for mixed-traffic work. No 30836 was one of five fitted with flat-sided six-wheel tenders for use on the Central section. It is seen here at its home shed of Redhill in March 1963. *Geoff Rixon*

*Right:* Revealing the parts which the cleaners failed to reach (and never expected anyone to discover!), this view of 'Schools' class No 30935 *Sevenoaks* was taken from West London Junction signalbox, east of Clapham Junction, on 14 May 1962. *Jim Oatway*

*Below:* Urie Class H16 4-6-2 tank No 30520 trundles through Weybridge in June 1962 with an empty coal train from Durnsford Road (Wimbledon) power station. The locomotive was based at Feltham shed along with the other four members of the class. *Geoff Rixon*

*Right:* The photographer, who would today be standing in a supermarket car park, captures 'H' class tank No 31518 leaving Tunbridge Wells West on an Oxted train in summer 1963. The Spa Valley Railway now operates trains from here and has taken over the engine shed. *Marcus Eavis*

*Above:* Brighton-built Standard Class 4 No 75076 awaits the signal to back out of Waterloo for Nine Elms shed in the summer of 1958. *Marcus Eavis*

*Right:* Britain's finest express of the 1950s approaches Orpington on 18 July 1959, hauled by unrebuilt 'Merchant Navy' No 35028 *Clan Line*. The first two carriages were for non-Pullman passengers. *David Clark*

*Left:* Drummond's 'T9' class 4-4-0s numbered 66 in total, all built between 1899 and 1901. Nicknamed 'Greyhounds', they became the oldest express passenger engines still in service, albeit relegated to lighter duties in their later years. No 30338 stands at Clapham Junction on 10 May 1959, still paired with an original eight-wheeled tender. One 'T9' (No 30120) survives in preservation. *Jim Oatway*

*Above:* No 30839, epitomising Maunsell's improved version of Urie's original 'S15s', hauls a Reading–Feltham freight through Ascot in September 1965. These express freight locomotives were frequently used on passenger trains. A number of the class have survived. *Nick Lera*

*Above:* 'H' class tank No 31177 halts at Brasted station as it propels a Westerham–Dunton Green push-and-pull in the summer of 1960. Today the train would be standing on the clockwise carriageway of the M25! *Martin Jenkins*

*Right:* Four massive 4-8-0 tanks designed by Urie were built in 1921 for the new hump-shunting yard at Feltham, hence the sloping side tanks to aid visibility. No 30493 has reached Nine Elms on 20 June 1959 but would be banned from Waterloo after one of the class became derailed there. *Jim Oatway*

*Above:* One of the final batch of 'King Arthurs', No 30802 *Sir Durnore*, passes Bickley on a down Ramsgate train on 16 May 1959. Like most steam locomotives on the Eastern section at this time, it is in deplorable external condition. *David Clark*

*Right:* Storming up the 1-in-100 gradient to Sole Street on its way from Margate in August 1958 is Class L 4-4-0 No 31766. This veteran from 1914 was built by Beyer, Peacock & Co of Manchester. *Ken Wightman*

*Left:* LBSCR 0-6-2 tank No 32474 leaves Platform 10 of London Bridge (Low Level) with a parcels train on 8 April 1963. The locomotive bearing the preceding number happily survives as *Birch Grove* on the Bluebell Railway. *David Clark*

*Above:* Built in 1921 for freight working out of Feltham yard, which they did for 40 years, the 'H16' class 4-6-2 tanks were also used on empty-stock workings at Waterloo, where No 30518 is seen in August 1962. *Bruce Jenkins*

*Left:* Shortly before the branch from Sittingbourne was electrified on 15 June 1959, SECR Class C 0-6-0 No 31495 waits at Sheerness-on-Sea while much activity takes place on the platform. Of the 109 built, one class member survives. *Marcus Eavis*

*Above:* With evidence of a light snowfall in the background, 'King Arthur' class No 30769 *Sir Balan* approaches St Mary Cray Junction on 26 March 1959 with an up Ramsgate express. *Ken Wightman*

*Left:* Uncommon (and certainly the ugliest!) motive power for a passenger train was Bulleid's wartime 'Q1' class. No 33006 enters Earley station on the Reading–Redhill line in 1964. *Nick Lera*

*Above:* Unrebuilt Bulleid Pacific No 34066 *Spitfire* simmers outside Woking in September 1965. Of the 110 engines of the 'West Country' / 'Battle of Britain' class produced between 1945 and 1949, an astonishing 20 survive today. *Author*

48

*Left:* This view of Guildford's distinctive half-roundhouse, taken from a passing train in September 1964, features the immaculate shed pilot, 'USA' tank No 30064 (now preserved) flanked by two 'N' class 2-6-0s, Nos 31814 and 31858. *Geoff Rixon*

*Above:* The LBSCR 'C2X' class comprised 45 Billinton 'C2' class 0-6-0s rebuilt by Marsh with larger boilers and extended smokeboxes. No 32547 takes water at Norwood Junction shed on 30 September 1961. *Jim Oatway*

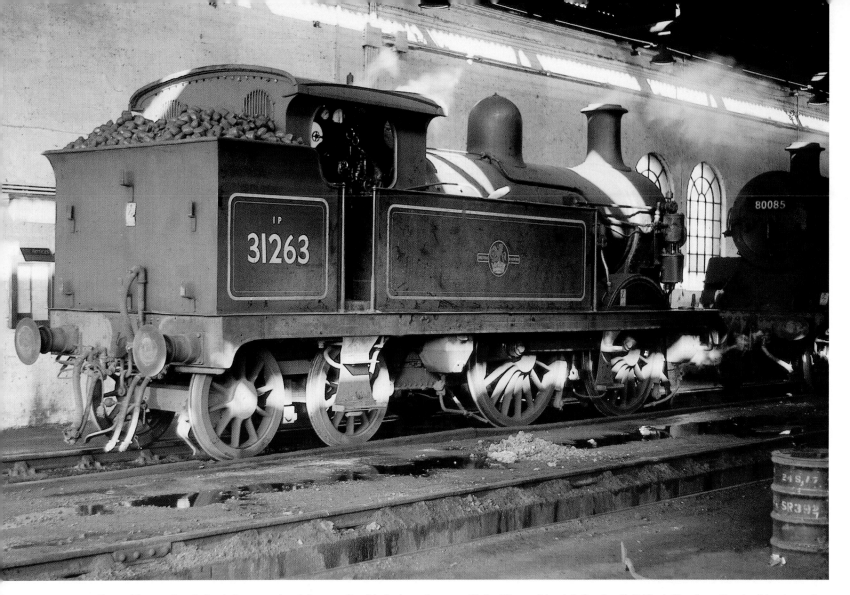

*Above:* The sun has indeed shone on the righteous, for this is the only 'H' class tank to survive. Seen at Tunbridge Wells West shed on 16 March 1963, No 31263 illustrates the attractive 'pagoda' style of cab roof, which gave extra protection to footplate crew. *Geoff Rixon*

*Right:* The end is nigh for the Guildford–Horsham line in this view of Ivatt Class 2 2-6-2 tank No 41294 leaving Guildford in June 1965. The line was an obvious candidate for the axe because trains were slow and infrequent, taking over ¾ hour to travel the 20-mile route. *Marcus Eavis*

*Left:* Eagle-eyed readers, noticing the size of the splashers, will immediately identify this locomotive as a rebuild of a 'River' class 2-6-4 tank. In the summer of 1962, Class U 2-6-0 No 31808 hauls an inter-Regional train on the Western Region at Tilehurst. *Derek Penney*

*Above:* The flagship member of a class of 16, No 30850 *Lord Nelson* works a down Bournemouth train through Esher in July 1960. This Maunsell locomotive was built in 1926 and is the sole representative preserved. *Geoff Rixon*

*Above:* With a section of streamlining removed, unrebuilt 'West Country' No 34033 *Chard* ambles past the closed Bramshot Halt, one mile east of Fleet, on an up Weymouth boat train in August 1965. *Author*

*Right:* The 11½-mile Hawkhurst branch penetrated the hop fields of Kent but lack of patronage caused its closure on 12 June 1961. SECR Class H No 31177 is about to propel a Paddock Wood-bound push-and-pull out of Goudhurst. *David Clark*

*Left:* SECR Class C No 31716, built by Sharp, Stewart & Co in 1900, stands at Wateringbury, beside the River Medway, on 2 June 1961 with a Maidstone West service. This station is a veritable time-capsule today, with semaphore signalling, signalbox and hand-operated level crossing. The station buildings are in private hands. *David Clark*

*Above:* Waiting at Shalford, near Guildford, on a freight train in September 1965 is 'N' class 2-6-0 No 31816, an SECR engine dating from 1922. Perhaps surprisingly, only one of the class has been preserved, compared with four Class U locomotives. *Author*

*Left:* More sharp eyes are needed to spot the fluted coupling rods which make this an 'E1' rather than a 'D1'. Seen at Paddock Wood with a down ballast train on 22 April 1961, No 31019 was rebuilt from an 'E' class 4-4-0 by Beyer, Peacock & Co in 1920. *David Clark*

*Above:* Clapham Junction station seems to be having a repaint in this shot of Standard 2-6-4 tank No 80088 on a Victoria–Tunbridge Wells West service in 1962. The former overhead signalbox is visible behind the back of the train. *Marcus Eavis*

*Left:* Rebuilt 'West Country' No 34012 *Launceston* prepares to reverse out of Cannon Street station and cross the River Thames. The bridge was saved in May 1941 by 'Schools' No 30934 *St Lawrence*, which was on the bridge when it was struck by a bomb. Despite extensive damage, the locomotive was subsequently repaired. *Ken Wightman*

*Below:* The up 'Night Ferry' from Paris to Victoria, composed of French (SNCF) rolling stock and headed by 'Merchant Navy' No 35001 *Channel Packet*, has just passed Shortlands Junction early on an October morning in 1957. Britain's heaviest scheduled passenger train, the service began in October 1936 and would be withdrawn in October 1980, a victim of increasing air travel. *Ken Wightman*

*Left:* Standard Class 4 No 80015 prepares to leave Kensington Olympia for Clapham Junction. For many years such rush-hour-only services were unpublished in the timetable. Just visible on the left is the unique glassfibre-bodied carriage built on the underframe of a coach destroyed in the St Johns accident of 1957. *Nick Lera*

*Above:* Bereft of its nameplates, the last working unrebuilt Bulleid Pacific, No 34102 *Lapford*, heads a down Bournemouth express through Weybridge in the final days of Southern steam during the summer of 1967. By this time the familiar green livery of the coaches was giving way to British Rail blue and grey. *Nick Lera*

63

*Above:* Working alongside the numerous 'H' class tanks on Central-section rural services in the early 1960s were a few LSWR 'M7' class tanks. No 30029 receives some spit and polish at Tunbridge Wells West shed on 16 March 1963. *Geoff Rixon*

*Right:* Pioneer 'Merchant Navy' No 35001, now in rebuilt form (see page 61), waits to leave Waterloo with the 10.30am to Bournemouth in September 1964. The platform canopies were removed in August 2002. *Marcus Eavis*

*Above:* No 30542, one of Maunsell's class of 20 'Q' class 0-6-0s built 1937-9, stands coupled to 'Q1' 0-6-0 No 33004 at Woking on 23 August 1964. Nos 30541 and 33001 survive today as the sole representatives of these classes. *Geoff Rixon*

*Right:* 'Schools' class No 30906 *Sherborne* ambles into retirement (and oblivion) in September 1962. This scene is near Farnborough North on the Reading–Redhill line, just before the overbridge carrying the South Western main line. *Derek Penney*

*Above:* The sole surviving 'H' class tank, No 31263, scurries away from Ashurst on an Oxted–Tunbridge Wells West train in August 1963. The splendid station building at Ashurst, visible in the background, is sadly no more, although this section of line is still open. *David Clark*

*Right:* Passing the new Shortlands Junction signalbox is an up Ramsgate train headed by Class U1 2-6-0 No 31905. This scene dates from October 1958, when track improvements preparatory to electrification of the Kent Coast services had just been completed in the Bromley South area. *Ken Wightman*

*Above:* A fine array of lower-quadrant signals frame rebuilt 'West Country' No 34044 *Woolacombe* as it hauls an up Waterloo express near Bramshot in August 1965. *Author*

*Right:* 'Q1' class 0-6-0 No 33006 is about to have its smokebox opened at Feltham shed in August 1965. Seldom were the Southern's 'ugly ducklings' found in such presentable condition. *Author*

*Left:* 'H' class tank No 31263 (again!) on a Three Bridges–
East Grinstead train passes 'Q' No 30543 at Rowfant on 12 June 1963,
four years before the line closed. The charming station building dating
from 1855 survives today, with the Worth Way footpath running
behind it and the platform side now situated within industrial premises.
*David Clark*

*Above:* Billinton's handsome LBSCR Class K 2-6-0s, numbering 17
locomotives, bore more than a passing resemblance to the famous
Brighton Atlantics. Dating from 1913, No 32341 was photographed
at Three Bridges shed on 1 April 1962. *Jim Oatway*

*Above:* The down 'Kentish Belle' — the 11.35am Pullman train from Victoria to Ramsgate — passes under Downsbridge Road, near Shortlands, in the summer of 1958. At its head is 'King Arthur' No 30795 *Sir Dinadan. Ken Wightman*

*Right:* There is no trace of Rudgwick station today, although Station Road and a new road — The Sidings — provide a clue, as does the overbridge (behind the photographer). This part of the Guildford–Horsham trackbed is now a public footpath. Ivatt Class 2 2-6-2 tank No 41294 is seen in June 1965. *Roy Hobbs*

*Left:* The second of the intermediate stations on the 4¾-mile Westerham branch was Chevening Halt. This view depicts 'H' class tank No 31177 propelling its train back to Dunton Green in the summer of 1960. *Martin Jenkins*

*Above:* Rebuilt by Beyer, Peacock & Co in 1921, Class D1 No 31749 stands at the former LCDR shed at Stewarts Lane, near Victoria, on 2 May 1959. This locomotive was the final member of its class to remain in service, lasting until November 1961. *Jim Oatway*

*Above:* Sixty of Bulleid's streamlined 'West Country' and 'Battle of Britain' Light Pacifics were rebuilt along more orthodox lines during the period 1957-61. Rebuilt 'West Country' No 34004 *Yeovil* hauls the 2pm Dover boat train out of Victoria station on 4 March 1961. This shot was taken from a passing electric train. *Bruce Jenkins*

*Right:* The winter sun is close to setting as Class N No 31816 approaches Earley station with a freight train on 3 January 1965. Between 1930 and 1935 this engine ran with steam-condensing equipment of somewhat Heath Robinson appearance, intended to improve efficiency. *Author*

# Index of Locations